African Elephants

by Shannon Knudsen

Lerner Publications Company • Minneapolis

Lerner Publications Company
A division of Lerner Publishing Group, Inc.
241 First Avenue North
Minneapolis, MN 55401 U.S.A.

Website address: www.lernerbooks.com

Words in *italic* type are explained in a glossary on page 30.

Library of Congress Cataloging-in-Publication Data

Knudsen, Shannon, 1971–
    African elephants / by Shannon Knudsen.
      p.   cm. — (Pull ahead books)
    ISBN-13: 978–0–8225–3483–9 (lib. bdg. : alk. paper)
    ISBN-10: 0–8225–3483–5 (lib. bdg. : alk. paper)
    1. African elephant—Juvenile literature. I. Title. II. Series.
    QL737.P98K54 2006
    599.67'4—dc22   2005011735

Manufactured in the United States of America
2 3 4 5 6 7 — BP — 13 12 11 10 09 08

What is this animal with the long nose?

This animal is an African elephant.

It lives mainly on flat, grassy land in Africa.

An African elephant's nose and upper lip are called a *trunk*.

How does an elephant use its trunk?

A trunk can pick up food.

An elephant uses its trunk to pick up grass, branches, and leaves.

A trunk can suck in water.

An elephant squirts water into its
mouth with its trunk.

An elephant may squirt water over its body on hot days.

The water helps the elephant cool off.

Elephants also wade in rivers
to cool off.

Sometimes rivers in Africa dry up in the sun.

How do African elephants find water then?

African elephants dig for water with their *tusks*.

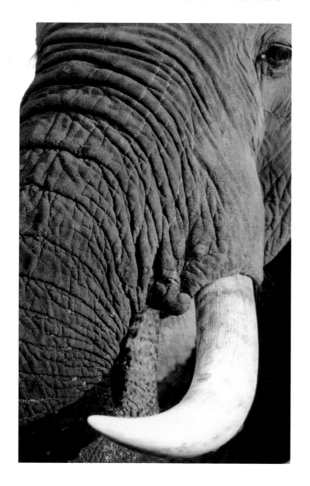

Tusks are long front teeth. An elephant has two tusks.

Tusks also help adult elephants protect their babies.

Lions and other animals sometimes hunt the babies.

Baby elephants are *calves*. Calves live in groups with their mothers and aunts.

The elephants in a group often touch each other.

They rub trunks or touch each other's heads to say hello.

Elephants also talk by rumbling and grunting.

They make loud noises that sound like trumpets.

Female elephants are *cows*.

Male elephants are *bulls.*

Usually bulls live alone or with other bulls.

Bull African elephants are the largest animals on Earth.

One adult bull may weigh as much as 70 men!

Big animals need to eat a lot.

How do elephants find enough food?

Elephants wander for miles
to find grass and leaves to eat.

Elephants spend hours eating
every day.

Young calves cannot eat grass or leaves.

Calves drink milk from their mothers' bodies. This is called *nursing*.

Most elephant mothers have one calf.

Sometimes a cow has twins.

Young
calves stand
under their
mothers'
legs for
safety.

Calves grow slowly.

They learn to eat grass and drink water.

They play with other calves.

Elephants eat and drink.

They walk and play.

Would you like to be an elephant?

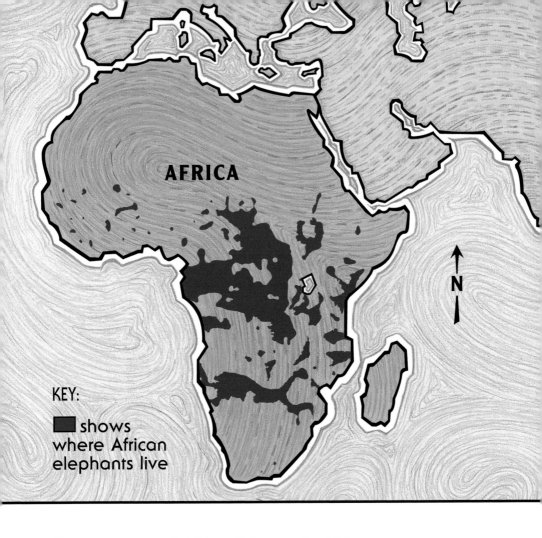

AFRICA

N

KEY:

■ shows where African elephants live

This is a map of Africa. Where do African elephants live?

Parts of an Elephant's Body

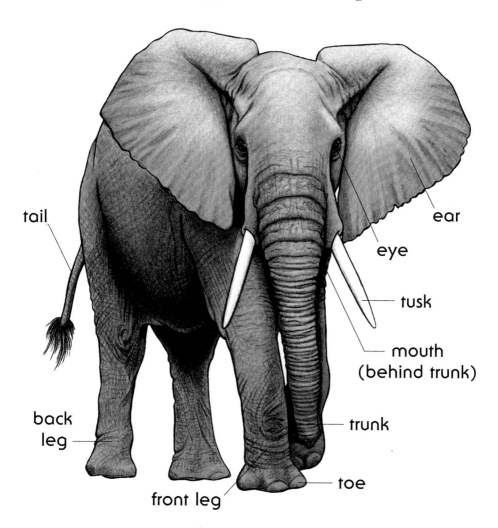

tail

ear

eye

tusk

mouth
(behind trunk)

back
leg

trunk

toe

front leg

Glossary

bulls: male elephants

calves: baby elephants

cows: female elephants

nursing: drinking milk from a mother's body

trunk: an elephant's nose and upper lip

tusks: an elephant's two front teeth

Further Reading and Websites

Donaldson, Madeline. *Africa*. Minneapolis: Lerner Publications Company, 2005.

Meeker, Clare Hodgson. *Hansa: The True Story of an Asian Elephant Baby*. Seattle: Sasquatch Books, 2002.

http://www.sandiegozoo.org/animalbytes/t-elephant.html

Index

About the Author

Shannon Knudsen edits and writes children's books. She has written books about mayors, the Easter holiday, and explorer Leif Eriksson. She lives in Minneapolis, Minnesota.

Photo Acknowledgments

The photographs in this book are reproduced with the permission of: © Sharna Balfour; Gallo Images/CORBIS, front cover; © Michele Burgess, pp. 3, 5, 9, 10, 18, 20, 21, 24, 26, 27; © Gerry Lemmo, pp. 4, 6, 7, 13, 23, 31; © age fotostock/SuperStock, pp. 8, 15, 16, 17; © Tom and Pat Leeson, pp. 11, 19, 25; © Royalty-Free/CORBIS, p. 12; © Kevin Schafer, p. 14; © SuperStock, Inc./SuperStock, p. 22.